CICE
R58718W0174

THE MODERN EDUCATOR'S LIBRARY

General Editor.—Prof. A. A. Cock.

MORAL AND RELIGIOUS EDUCATION

BY

SOPHIE BRYANT

D.Sc., D.Litt.

LATE HEADMISTRESS OF THE NORTH LONDON COLLEGIATE SCHOOL FOR GIRLS

AUTHOR OF "EDUCATIONAL ENDS," "STUDIES IN CHARACTER," ETC.

SECOND IMPRESSION

LONDON

EDWARD ARNOLD AND CO.

1924

THE MODERN EDUCATOR'S LIBRARY

General Editor—Professor A. A. Cock.

Crown 8vo. Uniform Cloth Binding.

Price **6s.** net, each volume.

Education: Its Data and First Principles. By T. P. Nunn, M.A., D.Sc., Professor of Education in the University of London.

Moral and Religious Education. By Sophie Bryant, D.Sc., Litt.D., late Headmistress, North London Collegiate School for Girls.

The Teaching of Modern Foreign Languages in School and University. By H. G. Atkins, M.A., D.Litt., Professor of German in King's College, University of London; and H. L. Hutton, M.A., Senior Modern Language Master at Merchant Taylors' School.

The Child under Eight. By E. R. Murray, Vice-Principal, Maria Grey Training College, Brondesbury; and Henrietta Brown Smith, LL.A., Lecturer in Education, Goldsmiths' College, University of London.

The Organisation and Curricula of Schools. By W. G. Sleight, M.A., D.Litt., L.C.C. Organizer of Training Classes and Adviser of Studies for Compulsory Day Continuation School Teachers.

An Introduction to the Psychology of Education. By James Drever, M.A., B.Sc., D.Phil., Reader and Combe Lecturer in Psychology in the University of Edinburgh.

The Moral Self: Its Nature and Development. By A. K. White, M.A., and A. Macbeath, M.A., Lecturers in Moral Philosophy in the University of Glasgow.

A History of Education. By Helen M. Wodehouse, M.A., D.Phil., Professor of Education in the University of Bristol.

EDWARD ARNOLD & CO., LONDON

Printed in Great Britain by R. & R. Clark, Limited, *Edinburgh.*

EDITOR'S PREFACE

THE *Modern Educator's Library* has been designed to give considered expositions of the best theory and practice in English education of to-day. It is planned to cover the principal problems of educational theory in general, of curriculum and organisation, of some unexhausted aspects of the history of education, and of special branches of applied education.

The Editor and his colleagues have had in view the needs of young teachers and of those training to be teachers, but since the school and the schoolmaster are not the sole factors in the educative process, it is hoped that educators in general (and which of us is not in some sense or other an educator ?) as well as the professional schoolmaster may find in the series some help in understanding precept and practice in education of to-day and to-morrow For we have borne in mind not only what is but what ought to be. To exhibit the educator's work as a vocation requiring the best possible preparation is the spirit in which these volumes have been written.

No artificial uniformity has been sought or imposed, and while the Editor is responsible for the series in general, the responsibility for the opinions expressed in each volume rests solely with its author.

ALBERT A. COCK.

UNIVERSITY OF LONDON,
KING'S COLLEGE.

AUTHOR'S PREFACE

THIS volume is written in the belief that, in order to produce the best result over the widest area, the teaching of morality through the development of religious faith and its teaching by direct appeal to self-respect, reason, sympathy, and common sense are both necessary. Children, like adults, differ much in range of susceptibility to each of these appeals. Some appear to understand little and care less about the direct personal and moral appeal, but are deeply stirred by the thought of the cosmic unity, of God manifest in the development of the universe, and calling each man to work with Him for its consummation. There are others in whom the cool analytic habit of intellect habitually prevails over the impassioned impulse towards a central thought. These have to think their way, perhaps with much labour, towards such a centre; and meanwhile the appeal to religious sanctions leaves them almost untouched. The claim of their individual human nature for a well-ordered personal life they understand: to the claims of social duty, brotherly affection, justice between man and man, they respond willingly and with intelligence. But they do not as yet lay hold of the idea that the purpose of God is the source and the end of their personal righteousness, in such a way as to have practical effect on them in these early years. Nevertheless it is, in the end, the pure in heart who sees all the goodness of God pass before him and, by means of the union with Divine Will expressed in that goodness, sees his way to God.

The modern student of paedagogy is familiar with the necessity of preparation as the first stage of the lesson. The Hebrew mind applied the same thought on a large scale, as we are applying it here, to the teaching of religion. "The preparation of the Kingdom"—so the Hebrew thought phrased it; and the Baptist preached it as moral righteousness, a getting ready of the mind for a higher flight, by practice in good works, in generosity, in abstinence from besetting sins. Indeed the whole trend of the Old Testament history points to inadequacy of moral development as the chief impediment to true religion. In every age this has been so, and surely it is so to-day. The ground needs to be tilled, the preparation accomplished by all the means that paedagogic science, philosophic insight, and common sense can discover.

SOPHIE BRYANT.

CONTENTS

BOOK I

SELF-LIBERATION BY SELF-REALISATION

BOOK II

THE MORAL IDEAL

BOOK III

THE RELIGIOUS IDEAL

BOOK IV

THE REASONED PRESENTMENT OF RELIGIOUS TRUTHS

BOOK I

SELF-LIBERATION BY SELF-REALISATION

CHAPTER I

SELF-LIBERATION OF THE SPIRIT BY WAY OF INTEREST IN KNOWLEDGE AND ART

I

"Truth, which only doth judge itself, teacheth:—that the enquiry of truth, which is the lovemaking or wooing of it; the knowledge of truth, which is the presence of it; and the belief of truth, which is the enjoying of it—is the sovereign good of human nature."—BACON.

LET us begin by considering the process of moral education from the humanist point of view. After what manner shall we treat the child so that he shall grow into the good man as good friend and neighbour? Education, as we do well to remind ourselves, is an undertaking in which the learner is not only co-partner with the teacher, but he is also the leading member of the firm. It is he, the learner, who has to grow virtuous dispositions, develop refined tastes, acquire the art of social life, and finally come to understand the goal and meaning of his existence. The teacher, or parent, is auxiliary; and part of his skill in that capacity consists in the astuteness with which he keeps himself, not too much but sufficiently, in the background.

The objects of education, in the intimate personal sense of the home and the schoolroom, ought therefore to be, as far as possible, conceived by us as objects that naturally make appeal to the learner himself, in the sense of being objects which he can naturally desire to achieve. The ideal we set before us at each stage should be one which we can reasonably set before him in such guise as will arrest his attention, interest his intelligence and fire his practical imagination.

Now it is of the essence of moral education that the child should, at an early stage, be encouraged to look outside himself for motives of his own activity—that he should get away and keep away from the life of self-concentration—that he should realise himself as an agent working on his world, interested in knowing it, and concerned also to find out what effects he can produce in it. This is the child's most characteristic relation to his world. Long before he is interested in himself as an object, he is interested in it. His awareness of himself is relative to his awareness of this not-self with which he plays, in which he finds a sphere for his activities, even before he becomes aware of it as a source of pleasure and pain.

Side by side with this life of activity, there grows up in him the life of pleasure and pain, drawing attention to self and, as intelligence develops, inviting his activity to manipulate his world for self-regarding ends. His inner freedom—the ultimate basis of his moral vigour—consists in his ability—his will-power—to turn a deaf ear to these claims of the sensitive self, and thus to maintain the primary active relation of the conscious self to the world. The healthy child has a great advantage over the weakling in this respect. At least this is so at the start, because the subjective distractions of physical *malaise* are absent in the former case. But a physical weakling may have that special quality of strong will—the innate habit of concentration on the purpose in hand—the practice of which is actually stimulated by the presence of opposing forces, so that it becomes habitually easy to conquer the claims of the sensitive self, and maintain, as against them, the ability to act as he deliberately purposes and wills to act.

It is natural to all ordinary children to work on themselves by effort and abstinence so as to gain more or less increase of freedom from these claims of the sensitive self;[1] and it is of prime importance that they should get all necessary encouragement and opportunity from grown-up people, and get it early. The defects to be guarded against at this point are: (1) the lazy will, (2) fear of pain, (3) greed for pleasure. As any one of these appears, the wise educator studies the case, and works steadily to effect a cure by personal encouragement, by the supply of attractive extra-regarding motives, by discipline in the form of insistence on the performance of specified duties, and also in the higher forms of responsible service as time goes on. These defects which show themselves early can be treated at once by steady persistence in the practice of overcoming them, *i.e.* by simply doing the thing which the spirit, if it were vigorous and free from the trammels of fear and the claims of self-indulgence, would immediately set itself to do. Any kind of practice to this effect is good. It helps to make the good soldier, the good student, the good citizen, in the long-run And obviously it is of the very essence of the good Christian that he should be that kind of person who continues his course when he thinks it right, whatever the consequences to himself may be.

This natural relation to the world of the Self, as acting upon it freely with a purpose in view, is highly favourable to education in every sense. Its loss is intellectual dulness, no less than gradual decline into self-regarding

[1] I well remember a very early stage of life when I found great silent satisfaction in despising cold, hunger and other hardships, without any particular reason for doing so. This ascetic temper predisposes, of course, to self-sacrifice and adventure. In delicate children it has to be watched on grounds of health.

narrowness of interest. Vigorous persons show their character by maintaining it under the most adverse circumstances. The educator clearly must not endanger it by setting before the child, as his ultimate aim, an ideal so suggestive of self-regarding motives as the development of himself for his own sake. The motive of self-improvement has its part to play—and it is no mean part—at a later stage of moral development; but in the case of the child it is better to ignore it as liable to misinterpretation, and moreover likely to be in general useless. Self-emancipation from the claims of self is the one thing most needful at the beginning. The child is not interested in being improved. His natural self-regarding motives are direct pleasures and the prospect of them; by using these wisely he can be improved to some extent, but not fundamentally. In the main, his natural primary method of self-emancipation is, clearly, by the extension of his natural extra-regarding motives—interest in knowledge, in making things, in personal achievement, in being of use in the world—together with the plain sense of duty and the kindly affections which his social environment, as well as his religious education, should call out in him continually. The abstract self-regarding motive—the calculation of self-interest, of which self-improvement merely as such must appear to be one form—lacks force and strikes chill in generous youth, as compared with these social, practical and intellectual motives in which he forgets himself, and escapes from the concrete self-regarding motives which arise in him spontaneously—love of ease, amusement, pleasures of sense and exercise. When a child is asked to do something distasteful "for his own good," the appeal fails in force, and at the same time, by suggesting self as the proper end of free choice, it tends to undermine that moral independence of self-regarding claims in which free spiritual life consists. For the spiritual life is the pursuit of universal ends: its outlook is away from self. To this thought we shall return later.

It would seem, therefore, that self-improvement in itself cannot well be made the young mind's first aim in education. To the child, at least, it should always appear with the social motive plainly at the back of it, so that he sees it as a duty which he owes to his world to make himself a worthy member of it, able to do it worthy service. In the meanwhile, all that any one might try to effect in the child's education—in the education of the race—is better done by giving room, opportunity and encouragement for the development of the three great extra-regarding motives—the interests in doing, in knowing and in social converse. And the cultivation of each of these—the first and the second as well as the third—has, since it tends to take him out of himself, a bearing on his furtherance in moral education.

II

Children love to know, and what they know they are generally glad to tell. In acquiring knowledge they are active and playful: in other words, they are so easily interested that they are easily distracted also. Moreover, the child's interest in an object of knowledge is in proportion to his power of getting any effective intellectual activity out of it. When he ceases to understand, he ceases to attend, and understanding is of course an act of his own intelligence, only partly related to our explanations or other means of evoking it. The child is, within the limit of his intelligence, more easily interested than the youth, and the youth than the adult. There are indeed adults who cannot be interested at all in objects unrelated to their established trains of thought. But the adult is less easily distracted than the child, because the object attended to establishes in him a more considerable and enduring train of thought.

The child's trains of thought are shallow and short. The important matter, therefore, at his stage is to cultivate his interests so that he comes to care for knowing what he can about the normal objects of human interest. Especially it matters much that the humanist interests in Literature, History, Geography should be developed early, partly because they are susceptible of early development up to a certain point, and mainly because the acquisition of the interest is, in these cases, even more important than special knowledge of their subject-matter. Little children under ten years, for instance, probably retain in the ordinary sense little of the information they acquire, but there can be no doubt that subconscious effects are produced which endure through life. It would be very instructive if we could discover what the subconscious effects of early religious education have been in different types of cases.

But our subject at this point concerns rather the possibility of creating a kindly disposed humane subconsciousness, in the minds of the little ones, with respect to other people in all times and in all places. And within the embrace of this wide subconscious friendliness, I would like to include all the planets that are sisters to our planet, and all the far-away great suns with the little worlds, like our world, that circle round them. Nor indeed can Science, in any of its branches, be excluded from the circle of humanist knowledge in the wide sense, so long as the Science interest is the pure knowledge interest in itself. This will appear more clearly in a later chapter.

III

In the second place, the child is essentially a doer. He wants to make things, and soon learns that, in order to make, he must understand the "How," and sometimes the "Why" of them. Thus the child's interest in making things may be used as a means to stimulate his interest in knowing all about them. Similarly, of course, where the practical bent is strong, it may be used effectively as a motive to increase of knowledge and intellectual activity. In any case, it is, like the intellectual interest itself, an important extra-regarding motive-force, tending to liberate the will from the dominion of mere self-interest—to deconcentrate the Self, objectify its activity, and thus facilitate its dedication to non-egoistic universal ends. The manual "occupations" of the Kindergarten, including the Sunday Kindergarten, are much to the purpose as means to the making of character, because they tend directly to counteract demoralising tendencies. The "occupied" child finds life full of interest; the idle one hankers after sweets, or cries about nothing at all. So it is also with the working man of all grades, if his work is so far in his own hands that he can take a real personal interest in it. The pity is that the conditions of modern labour tend to give the skilled artisan but little chance of realising himself as a producer, or part-producer, of some whole thing in which he can take a pride. Doubtless, the exigencies of the Great War have reacted on the efficiency of the British workman to such extraordinarily good effect in the production of war material, because of the stimulus to imagination which is implied in the demand for aeroplanes and other wonderful instruments.

It is certainly important in the interests of character building that the art-interest—by which is meant the interest in doing or making something—should, so far as possible, be preserved from letting itself be entirely smothered by the necessary interest of earning the means of bodily subsistence. Whatever makes labour — real labour to an end, not merely play—a living interest for its own sake is of service to the furtherance of morality. It is the dulness of life that drives men to drink, or to other mischievous indulgences and wasteful dissipations of personal energy. Inordinate love of pleasure in any form is a sign that, for some reason or another, interest in work and interest in knowledge are deficient. It is a good sign in the character of the French common people that their practical genius finds so much content in doing their common work well. Is this due solely to the genius of the race, or does it depend partly on tradition and wisely organised conditions which we might learn and imitate?

IV

It behoves the teacher, at any rate, to stand firm in the faith that—all variations of ability down to the lowest notwithstanding—every human being is in his degree a student and an artist: he does desire to know; he does take pleasure in making. By themselves, however, the practice of these activities does not carry us any way at all to the realisation of the moral end. If we use them in a vague and general way only, we are like the farmer who ploughs his land in the early spring and neglects in due course to sow the seed. Except indeed that, in most human hearts, there is congenital good seed, that will fall of itself into the ground and flourish all the better because this has been effectively ploughed. But let us dismiss that metaphor in haste lest it lead us into pitfalls. As a matter of fact, the child, no doubt, has all along been making trial of the third and more excellent way—the true main road—of personal affection and practice in social life. His knowing and his doing have attached themselves to and twined themselves round his interests in other people all the time. In this respect children, however, like adults, are very unequal, and some stand much in need of wise and careful treatment. To this subject we shall return in the chapter that follows.

Our purpose here is to note the truth that the art interest and the knowledge interest, like the social interest in all its forms, are important extra-regarding motive-forces, tending to lift the mind and liberate the will from the dominion of mere immediate interest in Self. Knowledge and Art may be counted, therefore, among the agencies that moralise mankind by liberating the personal spirit in individual men. Note, however, and bear it steadily in mind, that it is not the mere enjoyment of the results that follow on our labours — the agreeable stores of learning laid up for our amusement in leisure hours, still less the pleasure derived from contemplating works of Art towards the making of which we have not contributed —it is not pleasure in the results that carries us out of ourselves. It is the labour of intellect, the zeal of creative energy that is mainly instrumental in achieving this effect.

For the production of great Art and great intellectual achievement there must in modern times, of course, be an appreciative public which will make it possible for the gifted specialists to live. But this is not our present concern. We have to think more particularly of the rank and file of young people and the development of knowledge-thirst and craft-impulse in them. We have to think of garden-craft and house-craft, of the carpenter, the builder, the budding electrician or other engineer, as well as of those who have the impulse of the litterateur, the musician or the artist urging them to expression. Similarly, in the intellectual sphere, we have to think of boys and girls fascinated by the lure of enquiry into the wonders of Nature, or sharp-set with desire for knowledge about the History of the Human Race, or wrapt to self-forgetfulness in the study of Mathematics, or wide awake to interest in all happenings and conditions of the world as it is to-day. We have to think of all these activities as they exist for young people in our schools. We have to think of them as they are, and as they might be, at their best. And then we have to do our best, in homes as well as in schools, to supply, not too much, but sufficient opportunity to all children according to their possibilities, aiming always primarily at the development of the maximum of free-will and initiative in the utilisation of these opportunities by them.

The problem of combining this development of freedom in each individual with preservation from interference by him with the freedom of the others is that problem of perfect order in a perfectly free community towards the solution of which all well-considered schemes of democratic government must aspire. To this subject we shall return in the third chapter.

CHAPTER II

SELF-LIBERATION OF THE SPIRIT

BY WAY OF PERSONAL AFFECTIONS AND PUBLIC SPIRIT

"It is this effort to escape from one's own particularity and realise one's membership in a whole which prompts alike the search for knowledge, the creation of beauty, devotion to duty and worship of God. Man is a finite mind; but because he is Mind he cannot be content with his finitude."—*Mens Creatrix*: TEMPLE.

I

WE turn now to that third extra-regarding interest which is the moralising motive-power itself. That motive is the interest we take in other people, those interests whence come the pleasures of social converse, the deep happiness of close affection, the reverent admiration of the disciple for his master, the joys of hero-worship, the self-devotion of the philanthropist, the hero and the saint. It is the business of the educator to see that sufficient opportunity is supplied for the development of all these possibilities. An ordinary child, normally healthy and physically sound, will, if we study him, not leave us long in doubt as to the kind of moral opportunities he requires.

He loves to be one of a company—some children more continually than others, but all, or nearly all, children for most of their waking time.[1] It is natural to him to act and feel

[1] A little boy of five years came home to his mother after his first morning at school. "Oh, mother," cried he, "in all my life I have never spent such a happy day."

with associates—the family, the school, the little circle of contemporary friends—to be a part of a "We" and representative in some way of the whole. This tendency, which is the ground of human society, sometimes, no doubt, misleads the nobler spirits, as, for instance, among junior contemporaries in school who infect one another with conventional ideas as well as with sounder and, let us hope, more durable characteristics. Everything depends on the nature of the "We," not only in respect of the standards as to honour, truthfulness and fidelity it sets up, but at least as much in respect of the common sense, broad good nature, and generous kindly attitude which are shown by its members towards other "We's" and "I's." The family spirit may be detestably anti-moral in this latter sense. And the clique spirit in a school or college or any other large community is still more objectionable. The best kind of group is one which includes persons of all ages, with much variety of tastes, talents, social status, experience, expectations and intentions, who have some good common end in view, and who maintain a genial attitude to the world outside. The *esprit de corps* of the British schoolgirl is more catholic, perhaps, than that of her brother, to whom more ancient and less liberal traditions have come down. It is to her advantage also that, in her sense of the use of the first person plural, she generally includes with much heartiness the mistresses, junior and senior, of her school. The "We" should have all the dashing vitality of youth, the steady wisdom and courage of maturity, and all its characteristics should be toned to vivid interest in the highest human issues, and dissolved in the genial sympathy of that kindly human nature which is a thing apart from age.

But an imperfect "We" is better far than none. To substitute "We" for "I" is a gain in moral capacity, if not in the content of actual morality itself: and all experience of school life, and of life in a good-sized and well-managed family, shows how natural it is to the average child to live the corporate life and develop personal character by means of it.

It is much to be feared, however, that family life to-day is not the potent factor in the education of the children that it was some fifty, or even thirty, years ago. Middle-class families are smaller, and there is more distraction from home duties in the increase of interests arising outside the home. In respect, however, of the parents' fitness for their charge, it is probably true that, on an average of all classes, they have, but for one thing, more educational wisdom in these days than they had in those. The chief fault now, and it is a very serious one, is increase of over-indulgence and the relaxation of discipline.

But over against the Home there is the School. Great comfort is to be found in the thought that each of these two can, to some extent, supply the omissions of the other. The school at any rate comes into existence as an institution for the purposes of education solely: even if unaided by the home, it should be ready to fulfil the ideal of corporate life for the child. The family, if it were all it might be, could do it better: but, as things go, few parents now are able to make parentage the most vital interest in their lives. So we turn to consider corporate life in the school. All experience goes to show how natural and delightful to the child the school life is.

Two extreme cases have forced themselves on my attention. The child of abounding self-will, assertive, egoistic, finds in the life of the great school a field for his energies that at once sobers and stimulates him. He finds also, in good leadership and public opinion, a force strong enough, if wise enough, to draw him into a glad contented service, free because voluntary and very happy. On the other hand, I have seen wonderful effects of happy stimulus in the backward and insignificant—the unattractive girl, for instance, of small brain capacity, for whom there is little or no prospect of an interesting life just on her own account. Such a one finds a new sphere full of interest in all the eager life of the community about her. To her the "We" is so full of joy that the poverty of the "I" drops out of sight. It is good for a school—a girls' school at least—to have some such members in it—good for these girls themselves and good for all the others who are taught by their presence to befriend and uphold them, as they would a weaker sister in their own homes. Of course the weaker ones require some special help with lessons; but it is worth while to arrange for that.

II

So much for the sociable nature of the child and its training as a factor in moral growth. The next point to notice is the same child's readiness to respond to claims of service made upon him. This readiness should be looked for very early and utilised as soon as there is any service that the child can perform. I suppose one of the earliest useful things a child could do would be to pick up something that had dropped on the floor. There is no need to invent sham duties. Let us begin when we get a chance and not hurry. But, as time goes on, the wise mother will see to it that the stream of little home services from all the children shall be steadily maintained. It is in the second stage, rather than in the first, that love of ease and other self-indulgences set their snares. The boys should grow up to look after the garden, go on messages, and do odd jobs of carpentering, as occasion requires. The girls should have their allotted duties in the household work, including the family mending. Even after they all go to school—the day school, let us suppose—there is some time for home duties: and in the holidays they can make it their business to include their mother in the holiday benefit, by reducing the pressure of the household cares on her. For parents who are sufficiently well-to-do, it is an excellent plan to have a holiday cottage in the country, the service of cooking, cleaning, gardening, etc., to be run by the young people themselves. Those who are not well-to-do should have no hesitation in requiring similar contributions of service in the ordinary life of the house itself. All homes indeed should make their appropriate claim for service in some form from the children.

Up to a certain point service may be so much of the nature of play that the sense of moral obligation hardly enters into it. It must not of course stop at that point. On the other hand, there should also be a large field left for spontaneous services, little acts of unexpected attention, unsolicited kindness. In the end, as the social spirit expands and strengthens itself, all service tends to become a series of free-will offerings. The claim for service as that which ought to be—or even must be—done has, however, sooner or later to be made, and should not be too long delayed.

It should be noticed in passing that we here ignore all the compulsions "for his own good" to which the infant child is necessarily subjected: obviously they should be got through with as little nervous disturbance as possible, so that they may be immediately forgotten. Let us think, therefore, more especially of the child from five or six years old and upward.

The child, like any other living thing, adapts himself perforce to circumstances. The demands made on him by grown-up people, that he should do this and not do that, make up a considerable portion of the circumstances to which he has to adapt himself. To inanimate nature, *i.e.* the law of gravitation and other natural kill-joys, he knows he must adapt himself, and this acceptance of "must" is discipline. The hard outside world of people who know us not, nor care, is ready also with such discipline. The child knows well enough in one way, if not in another, that there are things which he must do. But in the case of an obligation which he does not like, laid on him by some one whom he loves and trusts, the sense of duty begins to emerge. He does not, let us suppose, at once desire to do the required thing, as a more amiable boy might; but his judgement tells him that he is to do it, that he owes it. "I ought" is substituted for "I must." The obligation is recognised as a debt of honour due—a duty.

III

Nobody knows, except possibly the boy himself, whether the act of obedience proceeded from the sense of Duty or from the compulsion of Discipline. The exact border-line is not, even for the boy, easy to determine, until by practice the duty-sense gets strong enough to stand out in clear contrast to the border-line attitude which might be described in the words: "I know I ought, but I wish I did not know it, and yet I suppose I must do it in any case." From time to time, the wavering sense of duty will be put to the test of a claim for obedience in the case of a disagreeable order or regulation, admitted to be right, which is made in the absence of all risk that disobedience will be discovered and punished. In difficult cases much depends on vigilant steady discipline, till this point is reached and passed. Thus, the slipshod, troublesome or shifty boy is gradually, as the phrase goes, knocked into shape. Afterwards, he, like his better-conditioned comrades, will set himself, at least, to do as others do in keeping the "rules of the game."

These others, more reasonable by nature perhaps, more friendly in temper and kindly disposed, have adapted themselves in a more intimate sense to the social demands, each in his own world of associates, the home and the school. By sympathy and reason—obscure no doubt and incomplete—they more or less identify their will with the source of the demands. Thus each of them moves because he ought—not because he knows he must. This is self-government under the sense of duty—one's own sense of duty—as president: it includes discipline and transfigures it: it implies a reasonableness, the borders of which in friendly human nature are enlarged by faith in the authority at the head of affairs.

It will be obvious too that the voluntary acceptance of duty, as that which is to be done because it ought, shades off by imperceptible gradations into the free-will offering of service given in the name of duty perhaps—but of the giver's own whole will. This may be because of affection for some particular person or for adventure's sake, or "for the love of God." But it behoves us here more especially to note that in a thoroughly socialised nature "I must," for the most part, becomes heartily "I will." In others, of more restricted generosity, it becomes simply "I ought." In either case the response is free of external compulsion, the thing is done with a mental reference—which may be subconscious—such as that "every one ought to do it," or "it was up to me to see it through." "Sure, it was only my duty," says a young soldier hero who had captured two enemy positions single-handed. "Hundreds of fellows would do the same if only they got the chance." To men of this temper, duty is just an opportunity for the exercise of a sublime free-will: the will of the hero is to do that which ought to be done, whatever the odds against him may be. And as the heroic temper works for this identification of ought and will from one point of view, so does the social disposition and "the love of God" work from another.

Duty indeed is one of the most natural things in the

world to a child, and the more so the greater his vitality. The strong-souled hate compulsion and resist it ; but their free-will service is given without stint. The obligations of discipline should be so administered as not to prevent the substitution for them of loyal service freely offered. Each young life, however, should have some claims of duty as such laid upon it, claims slight enough but steady, developing gradually from early days with the development of intelligence and the growth of self-reliance. And in this respect it is true that the children of the poor are often more blessed than the children of the rich. The poor mother may know nothing about theories of education, but she employs her little ones to take care of each other, and to help her in the home. Duties are scattered thick round the path of the bright-faced children of all ages in the cottier farms of the far western shores, while the denizens of the nurseries in New York and London are entertained with less wholesome amusements instead.

The atmosphere of duty is as necessary to the wholesome life of the school as it is to the healthy development of the child. It is as natural too as in the peasant mother's home. With large numbers there must be order, otherwise there can be neither ease nor freedom. If thirty to sixty persons in one room all endeavour to do as they please from moment to moment, the result is that no one can do what he pleases, unless it is to make a noise in a noisy atmosphere. After a little experience of this, children hate it. "How do you like your new mistress ?" said a little girl who had left school in a letter to her school friend. "Can she keep order ?" This is the children's point of view. Now order brings on the scene a host of little duties, simple and easy, well defined and not dependent on anybody's personal desire. They are demands made by the community for the common weal, and their appeal to the motives which underlie good manners, considerateness for others and self-respect should be transparent in them, and may well be made the subject of conversation in class when occasion occurs. In all this there lies a powerful, though simple and unoppressive, means of moral training. The life of a school should be instinct with the demand for such attention to business, such order in the production of work, such behaviour in class, such punctuality, regularity and diligence as shall conduce in high degree to personal effectiveness, to economy of other people's annoyances—to goodwill, good temper and courtesy all round.

And all this edification of character in respect of small things is by no means without effect on the development of the great virtues, justice, mercy, truth. If the life in a well-ordered school community be lived in faithfulness to the community, there will be no lack of practice in justice, practice in mercy, practice in self-denial, courage and truth. Faithfulness in little things builds up the character that makes for happy social order on the large scale, and for righteous personal life. The ordinary routine of school life, from day to day, supplies ample opportunity of walking freely in the Way; while for those who wander from it into a perilous place there is sure to be some one who will seek and probably save. The education of the duty-sense and the cultivation of the high-toned associate spirit on which so much depends are closely connected with the wise and careful ordering of the child's life while at school.

IV

Already we begin to see signs of the emergence of a well-wrought personality holding in control that chaos of desire and instinct, the sensitive impulsive self—"the carnal man." And this takes place not by an effort of mere self-control only, but by the steady direction of the child's activities to the accomplishment of ends outside self—ends with the sum total of which the ideas of duty and social service are closely associated.

The time has come now for us to take account of two more elements in the ideal of this personal progress. These are: (1) The interest of the person in his own Personality, and its development in accordance with some ideal of perfection; (2) the interest of the same person in the work which he will take as his duty and as the goal of his personal ambition. It is not, of course, in these terms that he conceives of these ideas in the beginning; but it is in some such form that they will appear to him in the end. He does not indeed wait till he has voluntarised and rationalised and socialised—in one word, spiritualised—himself so far as has been already considered, before he begins to start, with conscious intent, on making plans and preliminary excursions with a view to the two great adventures of the Personal Life—the adventure of making the best of himself—the adventure of doing his best in the world. Strong natures at a very early age begin to dream of these things; all natures which get a fair educational chance move on the same lines, in a more or less humble—more or less exalted—fashion of their own.

This emergence of the ideal of a good personality and its dedication to the service, and in honour of the "We," is the subject treated in the next chapter.

CHAPTER III

THE DEVELOPMENT OF CONSCIENCE AND THE SOURCES OF AESTHETICO-MORAL IDEALISM

"I am heir and this my kingdom. Shall the royal voice be mute.

. . . .

Hold the Sceptre, Human Soul, and rule thy Province of the Brute."

LET us take it for granted, as we certainly may, that some children care a great deal and most children care somewhat about being the right kind of person, as they understand rightness. At first it may be that they are entirely, or almost entirely, dependent on the approval or disapproval of their elders to show them the difference between right and wrong. That they have innate ability to make the distinction for themselves in the course of their development is certain, but there are two reasons why we must not in general trust wholly to this unaided self-development of conscience.

It is because a child has innate ability to disapprove a lie that we can appeal to him to set his face against it. If he has not the innate ability, he may, nevertheless, refrain from the lie in order to please, or to escape reproof; and, once the practice of refraining under good influence is set up and the ideal of truthfulness accepted, the instinct for truth-speaking begins to establish itself as a settled part of character. Under good training, vigilant and critical in respect of all shuffling and self-deception, the untruthful child in a friendly atmosphere acquires sooner or later a fixed idea that the telling of a lie is degrading and abhorrent. After that, if he wants to do it, the fixed idea confronts him—"pricks him." If he is in earnest[1] about being what his father calls a good boy, he succumbs to the conscience-pricks and speaks the truth. Without education in distinctions of right and wrong, few children probably would develop conscience in their childhood as fully and freely as they normally do, and many grown people's consciences would have pricks so few and so easily repressed as to be unworthy of the name.

Young children out of good homes are quite aware of conscience and much interested in a little real talk about it. They have no idea, of course, that so much of its content came to them from the wise, kind influences of other people calling out by sympathy the like response in them. What they know is that there is something like an authoritative inner voice, or guiding thought, that points out to them the way of righteousness, commands them to keep in it, and warns them against turning out of it, either to the right hand or to the left. The supreme fact is that conscience claims their obedience to right principles of action because they are right. To the child already carefully instructed in simple everyday duties it would seem that conscience, as a matter of course, reveals in all cases what should be done. But, as we know, this is not so; each moral agent has to discover for himself, with the aid so far as he needs it of others more experienced, what the content of conscience is, or should be, in new or difficult cases as they occur. *The mark of the conscientious child, as of the conscientious adult, is the resolve to walk in the right way, made with so much*

[1] This being in earnest is the inmost core of conscience: it marks the apex or growing-point of character.

earnestness, that no pains are spared in finding out what the right way is.

As soon as the child can in any particular see for himself the difference between right and wrong, this distinction should be emphasised in some way, as opportunity serves, in order to get the right choice made and the formation of the conscientious habit begun. Easy practice in its exercise is, at the first, more important than enlargement of its scope by acquiring more ideas of what ought or ought not to be done. One idea might be added at a time; the form "thou shalt not" of the Decalogue is, within limits, a very good form. There is a passage in the Church catechism which I have not looked at for many years. It occurs in "My duty to my neighbour," and is all I remember of that long and, as I thought when I learnt it, uninteresting admonition. I was probably about eight years old, and this is what I remember: "My duty to my neighbour . . . is to keep my hands from picking and stealing and my tongue from evil speaking, lying and slandering." The two great prohibitions of the eighth and ninth commandments, set out in such graphic typical, detail and with such fine literary point, are here illustrated in a practical and, at the same time, parabolic manner that is singularly attractive to the young child. "Picking" made me think of lumps of sugar in a bowl which one might first long to touch, and then swiftly to take: I understood perfectly that the hankering after the thing was the beginning of the sin, and that we must not interfere in any way at all with another person's property. Then there is the keeping one's hands out of mischief—behind one's back, perhaps, if necessary—and one's tongue quiet in one's head lest it should say what it ought not to say: I knew a girl once who used to bite her tongue on purpose when it threatened to run away with her and say rebellious things. In my case, it may have been that I had heard some teaching at Sunday School, or at home, on practical topics such as these, and the idea of conscience had gripped me subconsciously through them. I do not know; I was too young to remember.

There will be more to say of Conscience in a later chapter. It was necessary to say so much about it here, since its early upgrowth in the child's experience enters into his apprehension of himself as an agent with a personal character to develop, as well as a life-career to make in his world. The well-grown youth may be much less conscious of his conscience than the child. If it is a conscience that has him well in hand he may be hardly aware of it. The fact is, no doubt, that the leadings of conscience, which are derived from innate preconscious or semi-conscious causes, have made him what he is so far. Now, when he begins to think of himself as a person, he is moved to use all his powers of mind and heart and will, in order to raise his standard higher, and adhere to it more closely. But probably he will not look at it just in that way.

It is likely enough that the whole problem will appear to him at first in quite a different way, as a new problem to the interest of which he is just waking up. There will be others too—unregenerate so far—who wake up for the first time after this manner, saying as it were to themselves, "What am I? What am I going to do and be?" Even the young child may begin in this way; but it is not the best way for him, unless he discovers it himself, though he may ponder on it with advantage in his dreams of the future. Good material for dreams keeps out bad, and the child is capable of profound interest in his own individual scheme of life, as well as in his own individual character. Children—young children—like the men of bardic times are immensely interested in prospects of prowess and heroism for themselves; and this, of course, is more the case the more individualistic they are. The less sociable child in particular, who responds less effectively than is normal to social claims, is likely to do well under the treatment of good heroic literature in which ideals of chivalry appear. This sort of thing is always good, but priceless when we are little.

The test of the child's disposition to be interested in ideals of noble life and character is the delight he takes in the heroic element of history and romance. How do the different minds in a group of children react on the ideas of personality presented to them for instance in the tale of Troy? There may be some, the least developed in moral idealism, who are entirely taken up with the plot-interest. The majority, however, if they are not too young, will probably begin at once to look out for a hero whom they can acclaim as worthy of all praise. Hector, of course, always heads the poll in this case, but there may be other opinions. I remember one small mite, the youngest of the group, who turned them all over in her own mind, one by one, and, finding herself compelled by the strictness—not to say "priggish" rigidity—of her conscience to reject Hector, because he was on the side that had done the original wrong which caused the war, finally adopted Achilles as the best available, though below her standard in certain respects. The desire of the hero-worshipping child to find a flawless, or nearly flawless, hero is insistent, and indeed persistent also, in those on whom the idea of such a quest takes hold; and probably all children partake of this impulse more or less. It appears to be certainly an element in moral education to develop it and to turn it to its natural uses (1) in building up and clearing up the child's ideal of good personality, and (2) in stimulating the imitative impulse accordingly. We assume the existence of the warmth of temperament that blossoms into these twin impulses of admiration and imitation. We may count also on mutual influence among the members of a mixed group, in which some are delightfully warm and serve to tone up, by the outflow of their personality, the chilly reluctant tempers of their associates.

We come thus in sight of the definite suggestion that, in home-made circles as well as in the school class-room, place should be made for the reading of the fine old-world stories that go back to Pagan bardic times, each reading to be used as occasion for a conversation between the leader and the ordinary members of the group. The leader may be the parent or the teacher or the senior in the group. Sometimes, in order to arouse fresh interest, the members of the group might read in turn; but, for this kind of lesson with a moralising purpose, it is probably better that the leader should read and do it well, the retelling of the points of the story in discussion being undertaken afterwards by the children themselves. A teacher who tells a story well, will of course sometimes tell it rather than read it. The literary flavour of the well-written story is not, however, without a certain considerable value contributory to the attainment of the desired effect. Well-chosen words and beautiful phrases tend to the kindling of the higher lights in thought. The more nearly the well-told story—when it is told—approximates to its original literary form, the more effective will it be, unless there are special reasons to the contrary.

Apart from any definite scheme for moral instruction in this form, opportunities for such teaching as is here suggested frequently occur—and are used—in reading lessons and later in English literature lessons at school. If the literary matter under treatment raises, as so often it does, critical questions of character and conduct, then it follows that consideration of the text involves some discussion, direct or indirect, of these questions. The teacher, as mere teacher of literature, will be wise to give the members of the class an opening for the expression of their own thoughts. And for the teacher himself, it will add to his efficiency if his equipment in ethical interest and scholarship is ample and sound.[1] The important thing to realise in all these incidental teachings is that the social sense, the duty sense, the sense of personal rectitude and honour should develop together as one inter-related whole, by the double process of intelligent reflection and unremitting practice, both to be undertaken as far as possible on the child's own initiative. It is of no small importance that this initiative should be enlisted for active service on the side of righteousness before the self-conscious age is reached when the motive of calculating self-interest begins to assert itself. If St. George is on the spot before the dragon comes out of his lair, so much the better for St. George.

From eight to ten years of age appears to be the time when the foundations of moral idealism can best be laid by the use of stories from literary sources and also from real life. But we need not by any means wait till eight years old, and certainly the process needs to be continued later. Between ten and twelve, children who have been well grounded—as many are not—in the art of really reading a story or a poem, so as to get at the sense of it and meditate upon it, will be able to continue this line of their education, for the most part, by themselves. Probably they will not have the least idea that they are improving themselves—we must hope not—but if they have already acquired the great art of reading a story with dramatic intelligence and imaginative sympathy directed to the *dramatis personae*, they will not readily forgo the joy thus set before them for the sake of the much more transitory pleasure of rushing

[1] No one, in fact, is qualified to teach literature effectively who is, either by nature or for lack of education, deficient in ethical interest and psychologic insight.

pell-mell through the tale, intent on discovering, and not even remembering, the plot.

The grown-up relations and friends can be of great assistance to the children by wise choice of books when a gift time is at hand. In school, much use may be made of the lending library, if it is carefully requisitioned and used by the children, with just as much advice as they are glad to have from the teacher. Some children of course want more advice, others want less. Suggestions thrown out freely—talks about books—are good for all. As life in this country is organised now, it falls more than it ought to the school to provide a substitute for the kind of conversation and reciprocal flow of thought and feeling between parents and children, for which fathers at least in these days find so little time, except perhaps still in some peaceful country rectories and other havens remote from crowded towns. In towns, however, there are facilities for getting books from libraries—free libraries and others besides the school library—of which the elder girls and boys can make much use. It is possible, therefore, when occasion makes it desirable for the teacher to advise a whole class, or even the whole school, to read a certain book, that, in one way or another, they will all or most of them succeed in doing it. There is a delightful book of Mrs. Hodgson Burnett, *The Lost Prince,* which I read a couple of years ago. It is a story of two boys of twelve years of age, one of whom had been in training, with his father as comrade, all his life, to work for the accomplishment of some purpose known to his father but not to him. The other boy, a waif of the London streets, with the spirit of a hero in his crippled body, comes into the story at twelve years of age and is taken into the comradeship as aide-de-camp to the other. The secret is kept till the end of the story. The moral interest of it lies in the personality of the boys, their self-training for their work and the steady courage and skill with which they carry it through. At the close of the autumn term the head mistress recommended the book very briefly to all the girls of a large girls' school, and advised them to read it in the holidays. Some brief characterisation of its contents was given, emphasising the idea that they should study the story so that they should get to know these two boys. There were nearly 400 of them, and they nearly all reported themselves as having read it. The teachers for the most part read it too, and there were conversations on the plot and characters in most of the classes.

There is another thing the school can do if the good old fashion—as it seems to me—of prize-giving obtains, and the head of the school has the choice of the books. The first prize gained at school is the beginning of the child's own library; it will be read with some special sense of proprietary pride, marked perhaps also and, let us hope, inwardly digested: if it is a book that incites to reading again and again so much the better, but the great thing is that it should be a book that stirs the mind and sets it thinking. Another point to remember is that children borrow one another's books to read, so that a wisely given prize-book may influence a circle. Also the home people read it, and therein is the possibility of another very important circle.

These are some of the ways, apart from lessons, in which the school can help to make good literature a household word in the homes of the land. The little ones, who have already made acquaintance with some of the heroic romances at school, bring home in their hands on Prize Day, a book with pictures and a tale that makes one glow—a tale about gallant deeds and generous chivalry, the honourable foe and the faithful friend. Good versions of the old stories rewritten for children are to be had in these days, and they are greatly appreciated. For seniors, good translations from the Greek are available, and, besides Homer, selection can be made over the whole field of Greek dramatic literature. It is indeed in this senior stage that the Greek literature is most effective from the ethical point of view. Its early paganism is less exalted in heroic strain than is the primitive paganism of the early Celtic and Norse tales. Of course it is an earlier paganism, and these others, as we have them, may have absorbed some element of the Christian atmosphere in the process of being written down by the monks.

Celtic heroic literature provides a storehouse of material for readings and talks on this subject. Every one will think of the Arthurian romance, which ought in any case to be well known to every British child. Simplified versions of the stories suitable for young children, and well written, are easily available: all the fine old literatures have been treated in this way. There is something to be said, however, for using in the case of middle school children an abbreviated edition of Malory instead: it would certainly be worth while to try that experiment, as also the experiment of Pope's translation [1] of Homer's *Iliad* and *Odyssey* to which reference has already been made. Malory, however, and the Arthurian tales, as we have them in the modern children's books, illustrate rather the Christian knight than the Pagan chivalrous hero. It would certainly be worth while for the teacher, at least, to make himself acquainted with the old Celtic prototypes in the Welsh *Mabinogion*. The comparison of the older and the more modern forms, from the *Mabinogion*, through Malory, and onwards to Tennyson's *Idylls of the King*, would make a delightful literary study at a later stage—say in the Fourth or Fifth Form—of the Secondary school. This is a case in which it pays well to bring down two birds with one stone: it can be done. The literary

[1] Seniors will naturally read the translations by Butcher and Lang instead.

interest and the ethical interest are inextricably blended each with the other. They support each other also.

Then there are the ancient Irish stories, a very rich collection, recently opened up for English readers by the translation of the Gaelic MSS., which has been the work of the Celtic Text Society during the last quarter of a century. This collection includes, as its oldest and most precious possession, the cycle of stories that circles round Cuchulain and King Conor MacNessa of Ulster, the origin of which is referred to the Pagan Irish times about the beginning of the Christian era. This story is retold in modern English, with the minimum of departure from the originals, by Miss Eleanor Hull under the title of *Cuchulain, the Hound of Ulster*, and ought to be in every school library. So also should be the companion volume, *Finn and his Friends,* dealing with a later cycle which circles round the Feni or Fianna, Irish martial heroes of the third century, by Mr. T. W. Rolleston, whose work is done in the same scrupulous and critical literary spirit.[1] Slighter, cheaper editions of these and other old Irish stories suitable for children are also available. There is, moreover, a little volume by Mr. Standish O'Grady, published by Mr. Fisher Unwin in 1892, called *Finn and his Companions,* which contains a delightful collection of short tales of the third-century champions, Finn, Ossian, Oscar, and the rest. There is a tale here suitable for children in the intolerably self-assertive stage, telling how Finn, who was the mighty captain of the host, trained and instructed his twelve-year-old grandson MacLewy, and, by means of wit, affection and discipline, converted him from being an exceedingly competent young person whose monstrous conceit and over-

[1] These two books are readable universally: they are also suitable for study by older students, and will, in respect of their ethical interest and literary charm, well repay those who study them with care. *The Cuchulain Saga,* also by Miss Eleanor Hull, in the Grimm Library should also be mentioned.

bearing behaviour brought the whole host to the point of demanding his expulsion, into a self-disciplined, high-minded, accomplished hero, loved and admired by all.

His first lesson is relative to the boasting and complaints against the others with which he attempts to defend himself, alleging that they are jealous because of his superiority. The old man reminds him of the famous Cuchulain who was the greatest hero in his time, and also the best beloved; and this is the record of the historians concerning him:

> He spake not a boasting word,
> Nor vaunted he at all,
> Though marvellous were his deeds.

And at the end of the story we have set out a few of the precepts which Finn used in the instruction of MacLewy, and which were afterwards repeated to St. Patrick by Caelta, and St. Patrick bade his scribe to write them in a book with an order that they should be used by his people in the instruction of princes.

Here are some of them:

Pursue mildness, son of Lewy.
Don't beat hounds without good cause.
Don't censure high chiefs.
Keep two-thirds of thy politeness for women and humble folk.
Don't rage against the rabble.
Strive to hold others in esteem, and to like them; so the host will not be offended, though thou art loud and noisy.

Acquaintance with this kind of literature in some of its masterpieces would seem to be an almost necessary part of humanist education, the literary and the ethical interest running side by side and strengthening each other, as it is their normal tendency to do. The books that occur to me as best suited for our purpose are those of comparatively modern and British origin. Every one will think of some half dozen of Scott's masterpieces: shall we say *The Talisman, Ivanhoe, Kenilworth,* perhaps *Woodstock, Quentin Durward,* and, it may be, *The Pirate,* which I remember appreciating very much on account of the two girls whom I admired. One of these stories would well repay reading and discussing in class, say in a Fourth Form. The teacher could, if necessary, abbreviate by well-chosen omissions, but it would be better to do this while reading aloud to the class without books in their hands. Another way to save class time is for the children to read some of the book at home. If one book—say *Ivanhoe*—out of a group like this is treated thus, a standard begins to be set up for the reading of others in the same carefully appreciative spirit. The art of reading a good story well is in danger of being lost. It will be lost if it is not revived by wise educational effort in our schools, and, largely by means of their influence, in our homes also.